Redemption Song

Michael Rosé

Introduction

The idea for Redemption Song is based on the poem by the same name. Everyone has a form of regret in their life, but with the idea of the redemption song, it allows more of a celebration for the experience rather than constant self hatred because of it.

Acknowledgements

Firstly to both Andy Jackson (photographer) and Urania Brown (model) for helping with the cover.
Mr Guy (English teacher) who introduced me to poetry. Chris Harding for all his help. Finally to various members of my family and friends for their part in the making of this book.

Contact

www.myspace.com/mrose_poetry
mrose_poetry@hotmail.co.uk

ISBN: 978-0-9559839-1-7

Copyright © Michael Rosé 2007-2008

Biography

Michael started off his writing from the age of 16 as a songwriter, but after a short while realised that he he enjoyed crafting the lyrics to songs more than the music and began work as a poet. He pursued these early days of writing under the name "Forever Dying", being a name to describe the feelings and emotions he expressed in his early poems. Initially trying to find a crowd for his poetry, finding he was creating websites in an effort to show it to his friends.

Developing his style and love for the written word, he started to read about poetry and the poems of other writers collecting ideas on how to shape his work. During this time he was still playing music with Artisian.

After many years of putting together a catalogue of work, by September 2007 he compiled a self published collection of 35 poems entitled "Redemption Song", but with no great success.

Now with his second collection, "Echoing Reflection", incorporating poems that were written in the same period of time as "Redemption song", as well as others that have been written in the period since.

Contents

From The Beginning	6
Breaking The Cycle	7
Flowers By The Well	8
Failing Suicide	9
Letters Of Love	10
War Born	11
Asphodel	12
Echoes	13
On The Page	14
Teardrop	15
Fade	16
Inner Harmony	17
Ciam	18
After The Tragedy	19
Listening	20
Hour Of Our Death	21
Another Attempt	22
To The One	23
Redemption Song	24
Goodnight My Someone	25
Death Of A Nobody	26
Sirens	27
Amongst The Dead Flowers	28
Lonesome Dove	29
Just In The Other Room	30
The Man With A Message	31
Into The Fires Of Imagination	32
Moment In Time	33
For You My Dear	34
Beauty From Across The Room	35
Shade Of The Elm	36
My Final Acceptance	37
It May Never Be	38
Mute	39

From The Beginning

This is the start of my redemption song
But yet, I don't get to sing along
The words sit right in front of me
But yet I can't produce it vocally
I want to sing it for the world to hear
But my voice clenches up with fear
Does anyone really want to listen?
Where with my regrets should I begin?
Maybe if you read on,
You'll hear my redemption song
Spring from the words of the page
Of my life and my coming of age
Reliving the lives of my family
Because the one thing in life that repeats is history
Thank you for listening to verse one
Because this is the start of my redemption song

Breaking The Cycle

When I'm in floods of tears
Drowning in self pity
Looking back over my dreary life
Remembering all my victories and losses
Remembering all the good and the bad

But with no limits, no laws, no questions, no answers
Through the agony of life
To sweet surrender to your demons and defeat them through your own self destruction

Seeing is believing
And now I'm blind
Through pointless regression
Remembering my astral oppression, of ever dying mind

Mourning for the ignorant
Like a rolling stone, moving on to a new day and a new place
Breeding the infection
Feeling this rejection
To succumb to fear
Like a dying dove

When shadows fall, and night becomes day
I've survived the night,
All I can think of is you
Breaking the cycle is my only escape
Not to fall into patterns
To remove my face, and expose who I am
To finally end this charade
And to be fulfilled in your rejection

Flowers By The Well

Imprints of lost soul
Lost at the side of life
I'm down in a hole
Lost, looking for a reason for life

Within my decaying silence
I keep my skeletons hidden
But through a life of violence
Some things said are forgotten

And in my archaic ways
I live my life as such
Counting the days
Because living takes so much

As you see the blue sky
And night begins to draw
You must say goodbye
As there is no more

Moths I find comfort in
I know you're there
Because my life is yet to begin
And you'll always be there

I remember times we had together
And finding faith in Ladywell
I know you'll be there forever
As I leave flowers by the well

Failing Suicide

Birds chirping
A light breaks through
Signifying a new day
And I awake with a feeling
A feeling that can only be described as regret
Regret that I'm still here
Realising that last night wasn't a dream
A dream for my end
I had failed
I'm still here
Here to live on
But I don't want to live on
Death being so much sweeter than life
And causing less pain
Why do I feel this way?
Why do I fear to see another day?

Letters Of Love (A Questionable Fate)

I write this letter
In hope that you'll read it
In this letter
I express my deepest thoughts
I hope you won't discard them
I write this letter
In hope you'll understand my love

But I sit and think
What is the meaning of love?
Finding someone that matches what you want
Finding someone that you can call your love
By finding the flaws within them and changing them into the "one", and forget their ignorant errors

Can you really find love?
Is there such a thing as love?
Do some people enjoy the journey, and spend their lives looking?
Do some people settle for what they hope is love?

A questionable fate in my mind

War Born

A world of scorn
A world of hate
What a world to be born
In a time too late

There's always a lesson to learn
Or something to see
As the candle of time burns
The end will always be

Have you learnt the lesson?
Have you heard the voice?
Freedom or oppression
Make your choice

Asphodel

Asphodel
Blossomed from hell
Feeling so mighty

Grown for a queen
As it may seem
From the eyes of Aphrodite

Looking so pure
But awaiting more
Leaving with a trace of lust

No one knows why
From the sky so dry
And a ground made of dust

It grows alone
Like a king's throne
A masterpiece of sin

Giving us prayer
That God does care
And remorse shall begin

Echoes

Shy shadows
In a parallel universe
Where darkness rules
Where echoes dance
Where echoes dance
Where echoes dance

With this darkness
With shamans and shepherds
Losing faith in purity
Hearing the echoes
Repeating their fears
Admitting no more to shame

Feeling helpless
In the ever growing night
Feeling remorse for their ever losing sight
And the Prince of Wales diaries
For memories to cherish

But if walls called talk
They'd talk of times of love
That will echo through the ages
And lighten our lives
Hiding shy shadows
In their parallel universe

Mirroring our will to be
Reflecting our lives repetitively
Today, tomorrow and forever
Living our lives as echoes
With the same places
But different faces

On The Page

Inside my dreams
You're watching
As I lay my life on the page

The moon laying a hand
On my forehead to silence
My crying soul

Leaving my pen to fall asleep
On the page to dream
The infinite dream

Once in a lifetime
A rose in the mist
In loves warm embrace

The height of depression
My scenes are guided by
The voices inside me

Within the secret
Lays the sickness, to stay true
To the Sun

Within the sickness
Lays the remedy
Of silenced dreams

To ignite the flames
Of the martyr to lay sacrifice
On the pyre

Teardrop

I sit here, running thoughts through my mind
Memories of what was and now what's left
Feeling everything, but showing nothing
Wondering what pitfalls are left in my life
And which ones are going to finally break me
How much can one person take?
Before emotion engulfs them and pushes them to the ultimate sacrifice
Trying to hide the pain and fear building up in my eyes, until no more
And all of life's anguishes are released into one single tear
Trickling down the cheek of the broken man

Fade

I see the fading in your eyes
I find it hard to realise
What is it that's torturing you?
But what else can I do?

I keep trying to end your pain
But my efforts are left in vain
Please help me to understand
Please just let me hold your hand

I catch a glimpse in your mirror
All I can see is this sinner
How did I get this way?
But what else can I say?

If you haven't worked out whose eyes I see
This poem is about me
I didn't mean to start off this way
But what else can I say?

Inner Harmony

I exist in misery
I exist to make other people happy
I exist because you make me

I see no reason for this treason
I see no reason for the change of season
From the sun to the rain, and back again, and everything else in between

I don't enjoy this existence
I don't enjoy everyone at such a distance
I don't enjoy this constant persistence

Of everyone so far away
I don't enjoy feeling this way
But what else can I say?

My feelings stay inside, choking me
I can't express my feelings for all to see
All I can do is fake my inner harmony

From every pain in my brain and every stain on my soul
Will all come alive and consume me whole
Because at the end of the day, that seems to be your goal

Ciam

I hide myself away
In this circle of sanctuary
I hide myself away
Because you won't forgive me
Forgive me for what I've done wrong
You won't forgive me but you hear my song
I'll hide and pretend I've only done right
Because that's all you want to see in your sight
I don't want to lie to them
But I hide myself away in my ciam

After The Tragedy

Which tragedy do you refer to?
I've seen so many in my time
Everything from a new life to an old death
Both of which weren't fair
Both taken before I was ready
But I guess that's why they're tragedies
If they weren't that, then they'd be effable
Indescribable, at least not in so many words
But yet I survived
I'm broken, battered and bruised, but yet rolling on
Rolling on to my next tragedy
Before it starts

Listening

The first year of my life without you
A year expected to be tough
But tougher than expected
Unknowing, unwanted and under expected
I've done a lot of things this first year
Things involving my escape from the family, from my friends, from the situation and myself
But I hope you're still proud of me
Because now I'm without your guidance I need your approval more than ever
I hope you're listening
Because nobody else seems to be

Hour Of Our Death

A horror of the senses, between the day of our birth and the hour of our death

From the other side of darkness, bringing hope into the light filled macabre

Hope filled passion of the longing day, into the momentum of paraphernalia of creation

To explain the face of pain, to live and sacrifice
And know your name to live on in your shame

Walking into a mystery,
To create the fate for a reason to believe, to find comfort in the stars

And where shall wisdom be found?
With a scare crow hung like Christ, where hope hurts?

A tale of a broken heart, the night the phoenix gave up
Bring these words to an end

Another Attempt

As I write in this darkness of the world of shadow
I wonder what will come my way tomorrow
Will it be the love I need or will it be sorrow?

I keep wondering if I killed myself tonight who would care?
These thoughts in my head start to be a pain I can't bear
Because all I keep hearing are the taunts, kill yourself, I dare!

I walk down the road thinking of various ways I could die
I reach the end of the road and begin to cry
Because all the reasons I tell myself to live, are lies

And I'm sitting alone, thinking over my so-called "life"
Wondering all the ways I can think of to end this strife
Bringing up the courage to end it all and use this knife

To The One

I have no words
        But thoughts to spare
Thoughts of love and lust
        Which lead to repent and despair
I lead with thoughts of you
        Beauty, wise and fair
Perfection at its finest
        Which to others is unfair
With poetry in your eyes
        And a smile so beautiful
Not to be with you
        To me, seems cruel
A voice of an angel
        Leaving me as the fool
It's only a matter of time
        That I shall be with you

Redemption Song

Shadows fall
Within this pit of despair
Deafening silence
Fills the air
A redemption song
Screaming, we don't care

Between the myths and the reality
Lies what I long to find
An infinite muse
That infests my mind
Leaving me somewhere I don't know
Except that I'm left on the stone of rind

Why's it come alive?
Cried my muse
This Jekyll of myself
I try to lose
But now I'm cornered
As we begin to fuse

This road we walk
Is thin and long
The longer we're together
The more we do wrong
As we walk down this road
Singing this redemption song

Goodnight My Someone

I'm looking for someone
I don't know who it may be
Except it's my soul mate
For whom I'll search for eternity

Sometimes I feel I'm close
But other times I feel far away
I always wonder who it may be
But she'll be there on that beautiful day

I will search for you
No matter how near or far
Goodnight my someone
Whoever you are

Death Of A Nobody

There's no minute silence
There's no national grief
There's no statement on the news
There's no headline in the paper

Why is there no minute silence?
Why is there no national grief?
Why is there no statement on the news?
Why is there no headline in the paper?

A person dies
A life ends
A person cries
A life surrends

This is not a national hero
Nor a well known person
This is a death of a nobody

Sirens

I hear the sirens
Not the sirens from the shore
But the sirens indicating war
Not world war three
But the locals decreeing infamy
From the local establishment up ahead
I wonder which local is now dead
A local cut down in their prime
But I tell you what, it happens all the time

Amongst The Dead Flowers
(Dedicated To Whom It May Concern)

Amongst the dead flowers
Moments turned into hours
A life I once led
Now seems to be dead
In this world of tragedy
I can see each of our agony
Be we're drawn together
In a soulless bond that'll last forever
Finding a strange comfort in our haze
That always seems to last for days
But one thing I take from these memories in the mist
For once in my life, I exist

Lonesome Dove

A lonesome dove
With a lonely love
Crying with empathy

Living with strife
Throughout its life
Dying literally

Sitting alone
Upon its throne
Loving everyone it sees

Surviving death
To draw another breath
And fly over the sea

Wondering when
It'll see you again
And survive your reality

Just In The Other Room

It came as such a surprise
I hoped someone was telling me lies
I wish it wasn't true
Because now I miss you

You mean the world to me
I hope you knew, I hope you could see
I can't believe you've gone
I know I'm not the only one

I can't even think
Of a world where we can't have a drink
I've feared this day
In every possible way

And now that day is here
It's worse than I ever could fear
I know you're just in the other room
But we'll be together again soon

The Man With A Message

Fractured mind
With a wounded soul
Speaks of a message of hate
And a dead love

Speaking sweet serenity
Of the war against war
For creation is the aroma of the soul
And destruction is the odour of hate

Through the open door
Appears a man of wisdom
He speaks of the great world
And the Armageddon of man

His face scarred from love
From an almost tragic past
But still with a smile to show
With an angry persona to hide

He disappears into the night
Without any trace of his existence
But one thing to remember
That life goes on after hate

Into The Fires Of Imagination

Into the fire I go
To retrieve the embers of thought
And raise the art of alchemy

From pain and slaughter
I try to bring up the worthwhile
Resurrect the past and remember your lie

Intense pain of angels
With quiet weapons
For silent wars

Lost in a hail of gunfire
Pain seeping through
The cracks in my jaw

Burning slowly
I fail to find the good in this
And manifest my pain inside

Without an outlet for pain
I slowly die inside
So now I try to run and hide

Hide in the flames
And write my soft sermons
Of serpents and cancer

Within the flames I'm alone
No once can hurt me
To stay in my mind and watch the dead dancer

Moment In Time

I see the stars in your eyes
Shining the light of eternity
I see the moon in your heart
With passion in your soul

And in this perfect moment
There's nothing
Nothing but you and I
Lost in forever

A moment I'll never forget
A black rose turns to red
With a serenity in love
Knowing this won't last forever

Night draws to a close
I watch you fade into the darkness
And out of my life
Wishing one day we'll meet again

For You My Dear

Whatever I've done
To deserve this life
To hurt someone
And begin your strife

I'm sorry for this pain
I seem to cause
For it has left me insane
And left my mind sore

I thought and repent
For the pain I have made
And the time we have spent
Underneath my tree, underneath my shade

Speaking of soft words of love
Has left you in fear
Flying whimsically like a dove
For you my dear

Beauty From Across The Room

I am witness to beauty
We speak maybe once or twice
But yet I see a life with you
Whether, together or as a fond memory
Maybe both, who knows?
The sad thing though
I am to scared to admit these feelings
Admit these thoughts
Because I fear, like so many times before
You'll scar me
I don't think I have enough space on my body to be burnt again
So for now, and forever
You remain the beauty from across the room that I long for

Under The Shade Of The Elm

Under the shade of the elm
I don't feel so safe
Because all I feel is stares
Staring because I don't belong here
Staring because I'm the next victim
I came here to write, fight, recite
But all I feel is hate
Nobody wants me here
But I should be used to this
I may feel the looks of disdain, hatred and death
I'll only leave if they fulfil their hatred
Until then, I'll stay in the shade

My Final Acceptance

Upon my crimson altar
I lay as a sacrifice
Waiting for the heavens
For their acceptance

An avoidance of doubt
Shudders down my spine
Of maybe acceptance
That may never happen

My life of sin
Covering my silence
Which shall prevent
My final acceptance

The heavens may never open
For me and my emotion
But I can only dream
As I sit upon my crimson altar

It May Never Be

I haven't as yet held your hand and already I'm in love

I've barely touched your face and it's always on my mind

I just need to smell your aroma, and I'll know its love

Obstacles in the way, I'll have to wait for now

Because whenever it'll be

Whenever I get to say those words to you, forever together we shall be

But until then, it may never be

Mute

I have nothing to say
No feelings to express
No thoughts to tell
No dreams or fears
Emotionless state

The wind blowing by my window

Distracting my train of thought
Unable to portray my words
Not knowing where to begin
Or know if an angel has sinned

One day my words will come
To help me succumb to fear
And control my demons
But until that day
I'm alone with my pen

Michael Rosé

www.ingramcontent.com/pod-product-compliance
Ingram Content Group UK Ltd.
Pitfield, Milton Keynes, MK11 3LW, UK
UKHW041433180426
11947UKWH00007B/417